TRUTH AND GRACE MEMORY BOOK

BOOK 3

GRADES 9 - 12

THOMAS K. ASCOL, EDITOR

Published by

Founders Press

Committed to historic Baptist principles
P.O. Box 150931 • Cape Coral, FL 33915
Phone (239) 772-1400 • Fax: (239) 772-1140
Electronic Mail: founders@founders.org or
Website: http://www.founders.org
©2005 Founders Press

Printed in the United States of America

ISBN: 0-9713361-7-2

Unless otherwise indicated, Scripture quotations in this publication
are from the New King James Version of the Bible ©1979, 1980,
1984, 1988 Thomas Nelson, Inc., Nashville, TN.

Cover Art by Jonathan Reisinger
Cover Design by Kenneth Puls

Introduction

Dr. Thomas K. Ascol

A Word to Parents

The Bible teaches that children are "a heritage from the Lord" and that "the fruit of the womb is His reward" (Psalm 127:3). Each child is a gift from God. This makes you, as a parent, God's steward. He has entrusted you with one (or more) of His greatest blessings. He has given to you one of His highest callings.

In our day the challenge of parenting has never been greater. Too many moms and dads give in to the temptation to merely "get by." Simply making it through with the fewest possible conflicts becomes the goal. When this attitude is adopted, parents become passive and children learn to be manipulative. One of the saddest, most tragic sights ever to be observed in the Christian Church is a home where parents have defaulted on the responsibilities that God has entrusted to them.

Children are not designed to raise themselves. That is why God gives them parents. Christian parents have been given the specific, gracious duty of raising their children "in the training and admonition of the Lord" (Ephesians 6:4). You cannot be passive and fulfill this responsibility to "bring them up" in the proper way. Prayer, discipline, Godly example, and consistent, continuous, clear instruction are the tools that we must employ.

The responsibility to teach children foundational, eternal, life-changing truth from God's Word is laid squarely upon the shoulders of parents by the Lord Himself. Consider the charge that He has given to moms and dads:

> Hear, O Israel: The LORD our God, the LORD is one!
> You shall love the LORD your God with all your heart,

with all your soul, and with all your strength. And these words which I command you today shall be in your heart. You shall teach them diligently to your children, and shall talk of them when you sit in your house, when you walk by the way, when you lie down, and when you rise up (Deuteronomy 6:4–7).

The primary responsibility for teaching your children about God does not belong to the Sunday School or the pastor or any program in the church. God has entrusted this important work to you, dear parent. If you do not invest your time and effort to teach your children about God, be assured that someone else will. The television and theater will teach them that God, if He exists at all, is an irrelevant, indulgent being that is little more than a nice, kindly old man. If you do not teach your children truth and righteousness, be assured that there are a multitude of teachers in this world who would deceive them into thinking that "truth" and morality are relative ideas that can be shaped to fit anyone's beliefs or standards.

Your church stands with you against the false teachers of our age which would destroy the souls of our young people. You have every right to expect that sermons and Sunday School lessons will reinforce the godly principles which you are trying to teach at home. But you have no right to expect the church to take the place of the home. God has given to *parents* the responsibility of teaching their children divine truth.

The *Truth & Grace Memory Book* (TAG) has been designed to help you fulfill this assignment. The emphasis, obviously, is on memorization. Some modern educators have questioned the wisdom of teaching young children to memorize. Concern usually centers on the fear that the child is merely committing to memory meaningless words. This is a real danger—that we will be satisfied with hearing our children merely recite back to us words and sentences about which they have no real understanding. That is why parents must *teach* their children the material in TAG. Personal understanding should always be the goal of our teaching. But understanding will grow (mine has; hasn't yours?). Truth committed to the memory provides the building blocks for such growth.

Discuss the material being memorized with your child. This should be done during the actual memorization as well as at other opportune times in the day. Daily experiences and observations provide a world of opportunities to *illustrate* and *apply* God's Word. For example, the inevitable "night frights" which young children occasionally have, become wonderful occasions to comfortingly remind them that, though we cannot see God, He always sees us. Take time to *define* difficult terms. *Question* your child in order to discover the level of his understanding. When you feel that understanding is being achieved, *pray* with and for the child, including in your prayer some of the concepts just discussed. *Expect* your child to learn, and *rejoice* with him over his growth in knowledge and understanding of God's Word.

No matter what the age of your child, if you will begin immediately, and continue consistently, to teach them with TAG, you will instill in them a comprehensive awareness of the Bible's whole system of revealed truth. Obviously, the earlier a child begins, the better. But TAG has been designed to be useful to young people as well as to children and preschoolers.

Three primary ingredients make TAG a valuable tool in teaching our children God's revealed truth. First and foremost is the Word of God. Several passages have been carefully selected for memorization. Key Bible verses as well as longer portions are designed to introduce children to the overall scope and purpose of God's creative, providential and redemptive activity. The student who completes TAG will read (among other things) the New Testament twice, the 4 Gospels three times, Proverbs five times and the book of Psalms twice. He will memorize (among other texts) the Ten Commandments, the Beatitudes, the Lord's Prayer, 1 Corinthians 13, various psalms (including 119!), plus all the books of the Bible.

Why place such an emphasis on memorizing Scripture? Listen to the Psalmist's answer: "Your word I have hidden in my heart, that I might not sin against You!" (Psalm 119:11). Furthermore, consider the great promise God makes in Isaiah 55:10–11:

> For as the rain comes down, and the snow from heaven,
> and do not return there, but water the earth, and make it

bring forth and bud, that it may give seed to the sower and bread to the eater, so shall My word be that goes forth from My mouth; It shall not return to Me void, but it shall accomplish what I please, and it shall prosper in the thing for which I sent it.

God's Spirit uses the Scripture to speak to adults and children of all ages, calling them to faith in Christ and directing them in the paths of real discipleship. Therefore, as a parent who prays for the salvation and spiritual growth of your child, you must be diligent in teaching him or her the Word of God.

A second element in TAG is a selection of Christian hymns which are to be learned and memorized. Many of these are familiar (such as the Doxology) and can be learned by very small children. Others are not so well-known but are profound in their communication of biblical truth. In all, more than two dozen great hymns of the faith are included.

A third ingredient consists of three different Baptist catechisms, which are spread throughout the three books. The phrase "Baptist catechism" may sound strange to many contemporary Baptists. Some may even consider it to be a contradiction of terms. The truth of the matter, however, is that "catechism" is not a Roman Catholic or Lutheran or Presbyterian word. Rather, it is the anglicized version of the Greek word, *katekeo*, which simply means "to instruct." It appears, in various forms, several times in the Greek New Testament (it is translated as "instructed" in Luke 1:4 and Acts 18:25).

Obviously, then, anyone who has been instructed has in some sense been "catechized." But the word came to refer to a specific type of instruction early in church history. In the early church new Christians were taught the essentials of the faith by learning how to answer specific questions. Certain catechetical questions were grouped together and came to be referred to simply as a "catechism."

From the beginning modern-day Baptists (who emerged in the early 17th century) have employed various catechisms. Catechetical instruction was regarded as a valuable method of teaching both children and adults the doctrinal content of the Bible. Keach's Catechism (whose author, Benjamin Keach—a 17th-century English

Baptist—modeled it after *The Shorter Catechism of the Westminster Assembly*) was widely used among Baptists in both England and America. Charles Spurgeon (19th-century English Baptist leader) revised it slightly and reissued it for use in the Metropolitan Tabernacle. A modern version of this same catechism (*The Shorter Catechism: A Baptist Version*) is introduced in Book 2. A simpler one (*A Catechism for Boys and Girls*) is introduced in Book 1. Tragically, the best known Protestant catechism in the world is largely unknown to most contemporary Baptists. The *Heidelberg Catechism* has been warmly received and widely used since its first German publication in 1563. A 17th-century English Baptist pastor, Hercules Collins, modified this catechism for his congregation and called it the *Orthodox Catechism*. Included in Book 3 is the *Heidelberg Catechism: A Baptist Version* (edited by Tom Ascol).

Southern Baptists of an earlier day freely employed catechisms. One of the first publications which the Sunday School Board produced was a catechism by James Boyce, founder and first President of The Southern Baptist Theological Seminary. John Broadus also wrote a catechism which was published by the board in the 19th century. Lottie Moon used a catechism in her missionary work in China. It is only in recent generations that Southern Baptists have moved away from catechetical instruction as an important tool in teaching God's Word.

By learning a whole, well-constructed catechism a child (or adult for that matter) will be introduced to the overall biblical scheme of salvation. Such discipline will frame the mind for receiving and understanding every part of the Bible. A good catechism helps one to read the Bible theologically.

For these reasons, catechism questions are utilized in TAG. Combined with the other elements, catechetical instruction can prove to be a powerful tool in training our children to be strong in the Lord.

Much hard work has gone into the production of these memory books. Karen Leach and Judy Veilleux have spent long hours in deliberation and refinement in order to see this project completed. We have borrowed ideas from earlier, similar efforts that have been utilized in other churches. Specifically, we built upon an earlier workbook by Paul Settle which was edited for Baptists by Fred Malone and further adapted by Bill Ascol. Rather than further adapt their work, we opted to redesign the idea and come up with a memory book that would more adequately meet the needs of the families of Grace Baptist Church. Now through Founders Press, these TAG books are being made available for wider use. It is with much hope and prayer that homes will be strengthened, children converted and established in the faith, and parents encouraged that this training guide has been produced. May God use it to gain much praise and glory for Himself through our church.

How to Use the Truth and Grace Memory Book

1. Make this memory book something very special in your child's life. Emphasize the importance of learning God's Word. If you are genuinely excited about it, most likely your children will be also.

2. Incorporate it into your regular time of family prayer and devotion. After you have read a portion of God's Word, or some Bible story book, and have prayed, take a few minutes to work on a specific verse or question. Learn to sing the hymns together as a family (You can do it! You simply have to make the effort.).

3. Encourage precise memorization. If they are going to spend the time and effort to learn it, they might as well learn it accurately.

4. Be very positive. Try not to let the memory book become a battleground where a contest of the wills (child's vs. parent's) occurs. This *does not* mean that you let the child dictate when he will or will not work on the material. Rather, do not let yourself get into the position where you are violating biblical principles (by employing rage, sarcasm, ridicule, empty threats, etc.) in your zeal to have your child learn the Bible!

5. Date each step. Throughout TAG there are places for the parent to signify that the student has completed the assignment. Treat each one as a significant milestone and encourage your child to keep progressing.

6. Go at your child's own rate. Children, like adults, learn differently and at different tempos. TAG is designed so that the material can be covered as quickly or slowly as needed. Do not hesitate to move beyond the stated age levels. Remember, these are merely suggestions.

7. Discuss the content of the verses, catechism questions or hymns being learned. Help your child understand what they are saying. Remember, the goal is spiritual understanding, *not* mechanical regurgitation.

8. Review. Avoid placing such an emphasis on advancement that your child is tempted to utilize only his or her short-term rather than long-term memory.

9. Rejoice. Your child is learning Bible truths that some adults will never know. Thank the Lord for the privilege of teaching your children about Him. Be encouraged as you hear them reciting the Word of God and expressing important biblical truths.

10. Pray. Ask God to drive His Word deep into the heart and conscience of each child. Pray that He will send His Spirit to teach them inwardly the truth about sin and judgment, heaven and hell, Jesus and salvation. As you diligently teach your children, labor in prayer for them until you see Christ being formed in them.

11. Encourage other parents. We all need it. Make a conscious effort to give it. Training our children in the way of the Lord is a high calling. We are constantly tempted to neglect it. We all fail at some point and at some time. Resolve to be an encourager.

OUTLINE

The following is an outline of memory work from Book 3 divided into suggested age/grade levels. If you are not beginning with 9th grade, we suggest that you begin with the appropriate scripture, hymns, etc. for your child as well as with question #1 of the *Heidelberg Catechism: A Baptist Version*. The catechism is written in a systematic format with each question built upon those before it. The memorization of the whole catechism will expose the child to a solid doctrinal foundation.

9th Grade

10th Grade

11th Grade

12th Grade

9th Grade

Galatians 2:20

I have been crucified with Christ; it is no longer I who live, but Christ lives in me; and the life which I now live in the flesh I live by faith in the Son of God, who loved me and gave Himself for me.

Date: _____

John 3:5–6

Jesus answered, "Most assuredly, I say to you, unless one is born of water and the Spirit, he cannot enter the kingdom of God. That which is born of the flesh is flesh, and that which is born of the Spirit is spirit."

Date: _____

Proverbs 15:1–2

A soft answer turns away wrath,
But a harsh word stirs up anger.
The tongue of the wise uses knowledge rightly,
But the mouth of fools pours forth foolishness.

Date: _____

Hebrews 12:14

Pursue peace with all people, and holiness, without which no one will see the Lord.

Date: _____

Psalm 46

God is our refuge and strength,
A very present help in trouble.
Therefore we will not fear,
Even though the earth be removed,
And though the mountains be carried into the midst of the sea;
Though its waters roar and be troubled,
Though the mountains shake with its swelling.

Selah

There is a river whose streams shall make glad the city of God,
The holy place of the tabernacle of the Most High.
God is in the midst of her, she shall not be moved;
God shall help her, just at the break of dawn.
The nations raged, the kingdoms were moved;
He uttered His voice, the earth melted.

The LORD of hosts is with us;
The God of Jacob is our refuge.

Selah

Come, behold the works of the LORD,
Who has made desolations in the earth.
He makes wars cease to the end of the earth;
He breaks the bow and cuts the spear in two;
He burns the chariot in the fire.

Be still, and know that I am God;
I will be exalted among the nations,
I will be exalted in the earth!

The LORD of hosts is with us;
The God of Jacob is our refuge.

Selah

Date: _____

Romans 5:12–21

Therefore, just as through one man sin entered the world, and death through sin, and thus death spread to all men, because all sinned—(For until the law sin was in the world, but sin is not imputed when there is no law. Nevertheless death reigned from Adam to Moses, even over those who had not sinned according to the likeness of the transgression of Adam, who is a type of Him who was to come. But the free gift is not like the offense. For if by the one man's offense many died, much more the grace of God and the gift by the grace of the one Man, Jesus Christ, abounded to many. And the gift is not like that which came through the one who sinned. For the judgment which came from one offense resulted in condemnation, but the free gift which came from many offenses resulted in justification. For if by the one man's offense death reigned through the one, much more those who receive abundance of grace and of the gift of righteousness will reign in life through the One, Jesus Christ.) Therefore, as through one man's offense judgment came to all men, resulting in condemnation, even so through one Man's righteous act the free gift came to all men, resulting in justification of life. For as by one man's disobedience many were made sinners, so also by one Man's obedience many will be made righteous. Moreover the law entered that the offense might abound. But where sin abounded, grace abounded much more, so that as sin reigned in death, even so grace might reign through righteousness to eternal life through Jesus Christ our Lord.

Date: _____

Psalm 119:137–160

Righteous are You, O LORD,
And upright are Your judgments.
Your testimonies, which You have commanded,
Are righteous and very faithful.
My zeal has consumed me,
Because my enemies have forgotten Your words.

Your word is very pure;
Therefore Your servant loves it.
I am small and despised,
Yet I do not forget Your precepts.
Your righteousness is an everlasting righteousness,
And Your law is truth.
Trouble and anguish have overtaken me,
Yet Your commandments are my delights.
The righteousness of Your testimonies is everlasting;
Give me understanding, and I shall live.

I cry out with my whole heart;
Hear me, O LORD!
I will keep Your statutes.
I cry out to You;
Save me, and I will keep Your testimonies.
I rise before the dawning of the morning,
And cry for help;
I hope in Your word.
My eyes are awake through the night watches,
That I may meditate on Your word.
Hear my voice according to Your lovingkindness;
O LORD, revive me according to Your justice.
They draw near who follow after wickedness;
They are far from Your law.
You are near, O LORD,
And all Your commandments are truth.
Concerning Your testimonies,
I have known of old that You have founded them forever.

Consider my affliction and deliver me,
For I do not forget Your law.
Plead my cause and redeem me;
Revive me according to Your word.
Salvation is far from the wicked,
For they do not seek Your statutes.

Great are Your tender mercies, O LORD;
Revive me according to Your judgments.
Many are my persecutors and my enemies,
Yet I do not turn from Your testimonies.
I see the treacherous, and am disgusted,
Because they do not keep Your word.
Consider how I love Your precepts;
Revive me, O LORD, according to Your lovingkindness.
The entirety of Your word is truth,
And every one of Your righteous judgments endures forever.

Date: _____

Read:

Genesis   Date: _____

John   Date: _____

Galatians   Date: _____

Ephesians   Date: _____

Philippians   Date: _____

Colossians   Date: _____

1 Thessalonians   Date: _____

2 Thessalonians   Date: _____

Hymn: To God Be the Glory

To God be the glory, great things He hath done;
So loved He the world that He gave us His Son,
Who yielded His life an atonement for sin,
And opened the lifegate that all may go in.

Refrain:
Praise the Lord, praise the Lord,
Let the earth hear His voice!
Praise the Lord, praise the Lord,
Let the people rejoice!
O come to the Father, 'thro Jesus the Son,
And give Him the glory, great things He hath done.

O perfect redemption, the purchase of blood,
To ev'ry believer the promise of God;
The vilest offender who truly believes,
That moment from Jesus a pardon receives.

(Refrain)

Great things He hath taught us, great things He hath done,
And great our rejoicing thro' Jesus the Son;
But purer, and higher, and greater will be
Our wonder, our transport, when Jesus we see.

(Refrain)

Amen.

Words by Fanny Crosby (1875)

Date: _____

Hymn: Break Thou the Bread of Life

Break Thou the bread of life, dear Lord, to me,
As Thou didst break the loaves beside the sea;
Beyond the sacred page I seek Thee, Lord;
My spirit pants for Thee, O living Word.

Bless Thou the truth, dear Lord, to me, to me,
As Thou didst bless the bread by Galilee;
Then shall all bondage cease, all fetters fall;
And I shall find my peace, my all in all.

Thou are the bread of life, O Lord, to me,
Thy holy Word the truth that saveth me;
Give me to eat and live with Thee above;
Teach me to love Thy truth, for Thou art love.

O send Thy Spirit, Lord, now unto me,
That he may touch mine eyes, and make me see:
Show me the truth concealed within Thy Word,
And in Thy Book revealed I see the Lord.

Amen

Words by Mary Lathbury (1877)

Date: _____

Mid-Year Review by Teacher: _____
Year-End Review by Teacher: _____

10th Grade

Colossians 1:12–17

Giving thanks to the Father who has qualified us to be partakers of the inheritance of the saints in the light. He has delivered us from the power of darkness and conveyed us into the kingdom of the Son of His love, in whom we have redemption through His blood, the forgiveness of sins. He is the image of the invisible God, the firstborn over all creation. For by Him all things were created that are in heaven and that are on earth, visible and invisible, whether thrones or dominions or principalities or powers. All things were created through Him and for Him. And He is before all things, and in Him all things consist.

Date: _____

Hebrews 12:1–2

Therefore we also, since we are surrounded by so great a cloud of witnesses, let us lay aside every weight, and the sin which so easily ensnares us, and let us run with endurance the race that is set before us, looking unto Jesus, the author and finisher of our faith, who for the joy that was set before Him endured the cross, despising the shame, and has sat down at the right hand of the throne of God.

Date: _____

Ecclesiastes 12:1

Remember now your Creator in the days of your youth,
Before the difficult days come,
And the years draw near when you say,
"I have no pleasure in them."

Date: _____

Joshua 1:8

This Book of the Law shall not depart from your mouth, but you shall meditate in it day and night, that you may observe to do according to all that is written in it. For then you will make your way prosperous, and then you will have good success.

Date: _____

1 Corinthians 10:31

Therefore, whether you eat or drink, or whatever you do, do all to the glory of God.

Date: _____

Isaiah 57:20–21

But the wicked are like the troubled sea, When it cannot rest, Whose waters cast up mire and dirt. "There is no peace," says my God, "for the wicked."

Date: _____

1 John 2:3–6

Now by this we know that we know Him, if we keep His commandments. He who says, "I know Him," and does not keep His commandments, is a liar, and the truth is not in him. But whoever keeps His word, truly the love of God is perfected in him. By this we know that we are in Him. He who says he abides in Him ought himself also to walk just as He walked.

Date: _____

Psalm 119:161–176

Princes persecute me without a cause,
But my heart stands in awe of Your word.
I rejoice at Your word
As one who finds great treasure.

I hate and abhor lying,
But I love Your law.
Seven times a day I praise You,
Because of Your righteous judgments.
Great peace have those who love Your law,
And nothing causes them to stumble.
LORD, I hope for Your salvation,
And I do Your commandments.
My soul keeps Your testimonies,
And I love them exceedingly.
I keep Your precepts and Your testimonies,
For all my ways are before You.

Let my cry come before You, O LORD;
Give me understanding according to Your word.
Let my supplication come before You;
Deliver me according to Your word.
My lips shall utter praise,
For You teach me Your statutes.
My tongue shall speak of Your word,
For all Your commandments are righteousness.
Let Your hand become my help,
For I have chosen Your precepts.
I long for Your salvation, O LORD,
And Your law is my delight.
Let my soul live, and it shall praise You;
And let Your judgments help me.
I have gone astray like a lost sheep;
Seek Your servant,
For I do not forget Your commandments.

Date: _____

Read:

Proverbs   Date: _____

Romans   Date: _____

1 Timothy   Date: _____

2 Timothy   Date: _____

Titus   Date: _____

Philemon   Date: _____

Hebrews   Date: _____

James   Date: _____

1 Peter   Date: _____

2 Peter   Date: _____

1 John   Date: _____

2 John   Date: _____

3 John   Date: _____

Jude   Date: _____

Revelation   Date: _____

Hymn: And Can It Be That I Should Gain?

And can it be that I should gain
An int'rest in the Savior's blood?
Died He for me, who caused His pain?
For me, who Him to death pursued?
Amazing love! How can it be
That Thou, my God, shouldst die for me?

Refrain:
  Amazing love! How can it be
  That Thou, my God, shouldst die for me?

'Tis mystery all, th' Immortal dies:
Who can explore this strange design?
In vain the first born seraph tries
To sound the depth of love divine.
'Tis mercy all! Let earth adore,
Let angel minds inquire no more.

(Refrain)

He left His Father's throne above,
So free, so infinite His grace;
Emptied Himself of all but love,
And bled for Adam's helpless race.
'Tis mercy all! Immense and free!
For, O my God, it found out me.

(Refrain)

Long my imprisoned spirit lay
Fast bound in sin and nature's night;
Thine eye diffused a quick'ning ray;

I woke, the dungeon flamed with light!
My chains fell off; my heart was free;
I rose, went forth and followed Thee.

(Refrain)

No condemnation now I dread;
Jesus, and all in Him, is mine!
Alive in Him, my living Head,
And clothed in righteousness divine,
Bold I approach th' eternal throne,
And claim the crown through Christ my own.

(Refrain)

Words by Charles Wesley (1738)

Date: _____

Hymn: Revive Thy Work, O Lord

Revive Thy work, O Lord,
Thy mighty arm make bare;
Speak with the voice that wakes the dead,
And make thy people hear.

Revive Thy work, O Lord,
Disturb this sleep of death;
Quicken the smould'ring embers now
By Thine almighty breath.

Revive Thy work, O Lord,
Create soulthirst for Thee;
And hung'ring for the Bread of Life
O may our spirits be.

Revive Thy work, O Lord,
Exalt Thy precious name;
And by the Holy Ghost, our love
For Thee and Thine inflame.

Revive Thy work, O Lord,
Give pentecostal show'rs:
The glory shall be all Thine own,
The blessing, Lord, be ours.

Amen.

Words by Albert Midlane (1858)

Date: _____

Mid-Year Review by Teacher: _____
Year-End Review by Teacher: _____

11th Grade

Romans 1:16–17

> For I am not ashamed of the gospel of Christ, for it is the power of God to salvation for everyone who believes, for the Jew first and also for the Greek. For in it the righteousness of God is revealed from faith to faith; as it is written, *"The just shall live by faith."*

Date: _____

Galatians 6:14

> But God forbid that I should boast except in the cross of our Lord Jesus Christ, by whom the world has been crucified to me, and I to the world.

Date: _____

John 7:17

> If anyone wants to do His will, he shall know concerning the doctrine, whether it is from God or whether I speak on My own authority.

Date: _____

Proverbs 16:16

> How much better to get wisdom than gold! And to get understanding is to be chosen rather than silver.

Date: _____

Proverbs 3:1–13

My son, do not forget my law,
But let your heart keep my commands;
For length of days and long life
And peace they will add to you.

Let not mercy and truth forsake you;
Bind them around your neck,
Write them on the tablet of your heart,
And so find favor and high esteem
In the sight of God and man.

Trust in the LORD with all your heart,
And lean not on your own understanding;
In all your ways acknowledge Him,
And He shall direct your paths.

Do not be wise in your own eyes;
Fear the LORD and depart from evil.
It will be health to your flesh,
And strength to your bones.

Honor the LORD with your possessions,
And with the firstfruits of all your increase;
So your barns will be filled with plenty,
And your vats will overflow with new wine.

My son, do not despise the chastening of the LORD,
Nor detest His correction;
For whom the LORD loves He corrects,
Just as a father the son in whom he delights.

Happy is the man who finds wisdom,
And the man who gains understanding.

Date: _____

1 Corinthians 10:13

No temptation has overtaken you except such as is common to man; but God is faithful, who will not allow you to be tempted beyond what you are able, but with the temptation will also make the way of escape, that you may be able to bear it.

Date: _____

Review:

Psalm 119　　　　　　　Date: _____

Read:

Psalms　　　　　　　　Date: _____

Proverbs　　　　　　　Date: _____

Matthew　　　　　　　Date: _____

Mark　　　　　　　　　Date: _____

Luke　　　　　　　　　Date: _____

John　　　　　　　　　Date: _____

Hymn: All People That on Earth Do Dwell

All people that on earth do dwell,
Sing to the Lord with cheerful voice;
Him serve with fear, His praise forthtell,
Come ye before Him and rejoice.

The Lord ye know is God indeed;
Without our aid He did us make;
We are His folk, He doth us feed,
And for His sheep He doth us take.

O enter then His gates with praise,
Approach with joy His courts unto;
Praise, laud and bless His name always,
For it is seemly so to do.

For why? The Lord our God is good,
His mercy is forever sure;
His truth at all times firmly stood,
And shall from age to age endure.

Amen.

Words by William Kethe (1561) from Psalm 100

Date: _____

Hymn: Great God of Wonders!

Great God of wonders! All Thy ways
Are matchless, Godlike, and divine;
But the fair glories of Thy grace
More Godlike and unrivaled shine,
More Godlike and unrivaled shine.

Refrain:
Who is a pard'ning God like Thee?
Or who has grace so rich and free?
Or who has grace so rich and free?

In wonder lost, with trembling joy,
We take the pardon of our God:
Pardon for crimes of deepest dye,
A pardon bought with Jesus' blood,
A pardon bought with Jesus' blood.

(Refrain)

O may this strange, this matchless grace,
This Godlike miracle of love,
Fill the whole earth with grateful praise,
And all th' angelic choirs above,
And all th' angelic choirs above.

(Refrain)

Words by Samuel Davies (1723–1761)

Date: _____

Mid-Year Review by Teacher: _____
Year-End Review by Teacher: _____

12th Grade

Matthew 25:31–40

When the Son of Man comes in His glory, and all the holy angels with Him, then He will sit on the throne of His glory. All the nations will be gathered before Him, and He will separate them one from another, as a shepherd divides his sheep from the goats. And He will set the sheep on His right hand, but the goats on the left. Then the King will say to those on His right hand, "Come, you blessed of My Father, inherit the kingdom prepared for you from the foundation of the world: for I was hungry and you gave Me food; I was thirsty and you gave Me drink; I was a stranger and you took Me in; I was naked and you clothed Me; I was sick and you visited Me; I was in prison and you came to Me." Then the righteous will answer Him, saying, "Lord, when did we see You hungry and feed You, or thirsty and give You drink? When did we see You a stranger and take You in, or naked and clothe You? Or when did we see You sick, or in prison, and come to You?" And the King will answer and say to them, "Assuredly, I say to you, inasmuch as you did it to one of the least of these My brethren, you did it to Me."

Date: _____

Colossians 3:1–4

If then you were raised with Christ, seek those things which are above, where Christ is, sitting at the right hand of God. Set your mind on things above, not on things on the earth. For you died, and your life is hidden with Christ in God. When Christ who is our life appears, then you also will appear with Him in glory.

Date: _____

Romans 12:1–2

I beseech you therefore, brethren, by the mercies of God, that you present your bodies a living sacrifice, holy, acceptable to God, which is your reasonable service. And do not be conformed to this world, but be transformed by the renewing of your mind, that you may prove what is that good and acceptable and perfect will of God.

Date: _____

Psalm 1

Blessed is the man
Who walks not in the counsel of the ungodly,
Nor stands in the path of sinners,
Nor sits in the seat of the scornful;
But his delight is in the law of the LORD,
And in His law he meditates day and night.
He shall be like a tree
Planted by the rivers of water,
That brings forth its fruit in its season,
Whose leaf also shall not wither;
And whatever he does shall prosper.

The ungodly are not so,
But are like the chaff which the wind drives away.
Therefore the ungodly shall not stand in the judgment,
Nor sinners in the congregation of the righteous.

For the LORD knows the way of the righteous,
But the way of the ungodly shall perish.

Date: _____

Proverbs 22:1

A good name is to be chosen rather than great riches,
Loving favor rather than silver and gold.

Date: _____

Review:

Psalm 119   Date: _____

Read:

Psalms   Date: _____

Proverbs   Date: _____

Matthew   Date: _____

Mark   Date: _____

Luke   Date: _____

John   Date: _____

Acts   Date: _____

Romans   Date: _____

1 Corinthians   Date: _____

2 Corinthians   Date: _____

Galatians   Date: _____

Ephesians   Date: _____

Philippians   Date: _____

Colossians   Date: _____

1 Thessalonians   Date: _____

2 Thessalonians   Date: _____

1 Timothy   Date: _____

2 Timothy   Date: _____

Titus   Date: _____

Philemon   Date: _____

Hebrews   Date: _____

James   Date: _____

1 Peter   Date: _____

2 Peter   Date: _____

1 John   Date: _____

2 John   Date: _____

3 John   Date: _____

Jude   Date: _____

Revelation   Date: _____

Hymn: How Sad Our State by Nature Is!

How sad our state by nature is!
Our sin, how deep it stains!
And Satan binds our captive minds,
Fast in his slavish chains.

But there's a voice of sovereign grace,
Sounds from the sacred word;
"Ho! Ye despairing sinners, come,
And trust upon the Lord."

My soul obeys th' almighty call,
And runs to this relief;
I would believe thy promise, Lord;
Oh! Help my unbelief.

To the dear fountain of Thy blood,
Incarnate God, I fly;
Here let me wash my spotted soul
From crimes of deepest dye.

Stretch out Thine arm, victorious King,
My reigning sins subdue;
Drive the old Dragon from his seat,
With all his hellish crew.

A guilty, weak, and helpless worm,
On Thy kind arms I fall:
Be Thou my strength and righteousness,
My Jesus and My All.

Words by Isaac Watts (1707)

Date: _____

Hymn: Not What My Hands Have Done

Not what my hands have done,
Can save my guilty soul;
Not what my toiling flesh has borne
Can make my spirit whole.
Not what I feel or do
Can give me peace with God;
Not all my prayers and sighs and tears
Can bear my awful load.

Thy work alone, O Christ,
Can ease this weight of sin;
Thy blood alone, O Lamb of God,
Can give me peace within.
Thy love to me, O God,
Not mine, O Lord, to Thee,
Can rid me of this dark unrest
And set my spirit free.

Thy grace alone, O God,
To me can pardon speak;
Thy power alone, O Son of God,
Can this sore bondage break.
No other work, save Thine,
No other blood will do;
No strength, save that which is divine,
Can bear me safely through.

I bless the Christ of God;
I rest on love divine;
And with unfalt'ring lip and heart,
I call this Savior mine.

His cross dispels each doubt;
I bury in His tomb
Each thought of unbelief and fear,
Each ling'ring shade of gloom.

I praise the God of grace,
I trust His truth and might;
He calls me His, I call Him mine,
My God, my joy, my light.
'Tis He who saveth me,
And freely pardon gives;
I love because He loveth me,
I live because He lives.

Words by Horatius Bonar (1808–1889)

Date: _____

Mid-Year Review by Teacher: _____
Year-End Review by Teacher: _____

Heidelberg Catechism: A Baptist Version

1. **What is your only comfort in life and in death?**
That I am not my own, but belong–body and soul, in life and in death–to my faithful Savior Jesus Christ. He has fully paid for all my sins with His precious blood, and has set me free from the tyranny of the devil. He also watches over me in such a way that not a hair can fall from my head without the will of my Father in heaven; in fact, all things must work together for my salvation. Because I belong to Him, Christ, by His Holy Spirit, assures me of eternal life and makes me whole-heartedly willing and ready from now on to live for Him.

(1 Corinthians 6:19, 20; Romans 14:7–9; 1 Corinthians 3:23; Titus 2:14; 1 Peter 1:18, 19; 1 John 1:7–9; 2:2; John 8:34–36; Hebrews 2:14, 15; 1 John 3:1–11; John 6:39, 40; 10:27–30; 2 Thessalonians 3:3; 1 Peter 1:5; Matthew 10:29–31; Luke 21:16–18; Romans 8:28; 8:15, 16; 2 Corinthians 1:21, 22; 5:5; Ephesians 1:13, 14; Romans 8:1–17)

Date: _____

2. **What must you know to live and die in the joy of this comfort?**
Three things: first, how great my sin and misery are; second, how I am set free from all my sins and misery; third, how I am to thank God for such deliverance.

(Romans 3:9; 10; 1 John 1:10; John 17:3; Acts 4:12; 10:43; Matthew 5:16; Romans 6:13; Ephesians 5:8–10; 2 Timothy 2:15; 1 Peter 2:9, 10)

Date: _____

3. **How do you come to know your misery?**
The law of God tells me.

(Romans 3:20; 7:7–25)

Date: _____

4. **What does God's law require of us?**
Christ teaches us this in summary in Matthew 22—You shall love the Lord your God with all your heart, with all your soul, and with all your mind. This is the great and first commandment. And a second is like it, you shall love your neighbor as yourself. On these two commandments hang all the law and the prophets.

(Deuteronomy 6:5; Leviticus 19:18)

Date: _____

5. **Can you live up to all this perfectly?**
No. I have a natural tendency to hate God and my neighbor.

(Romans 3:9–20, 23; 1 John 1:8, 10; Genesis 6:5; Jeremiah 17:9; Romans 7:23, 24; 8:7; Ephesians 2:1–3; Titus 3:3)

Date: _____

6. **Did God create man wicked and perverse?**
No. God created man good, and in His own image, that is, in true righteousness and holiness, so that he might truly know God his creator, love Him with all his heart, and live with Him in eternal happiness for His praise and glory.

(Genesis 1:31; 1:26, 27; Ephesians 4:24; Colossians 3:10; Psalm 8)

Date: _____

7. **Then where does man's corrupt nature come from?**
    From the fall and disobedience of our first parents, Adam and Eve, in Paradise. This fall has so poisoned our nature that we are all born sinners—corrupt from conception on.

    (Genesis 3; Romans 5:12, 18, 19; Psalm 51:5)

    Date: _____

8. **But are we so corrupt that we are totally unable to do any good and inclined toward all evil?**
    Yes, unless we are born again, by the Spirit of God.

    (Genesis 6:5; 8:21; Job 14:4; Isaiah 53:6; John 3:3–5)

    Date: _____

9. **But doesn't God do man an injustice by requiring in His law what man is unable to do?**
    No, God created man with the ability to keep the law. Man, however, when tempted by the devil, in reckless disobedience, robbed himself and his descendants of these gifts.

    (Genesis 1:31; Ephesians 4:24; Genesis 3:13; John 8:44; Genesis 3:6; Romans 5:12, 18, 19)

    Date: _____

10. **Will God permit such disobedience and rebellion to go unpunished?**
    Certainly not. He is terribly angry about the sin we are born with as well as the sins we personally commit. As a just judge He punishes them now and in eternity. He has declared: "Cursed is the one who does not confirm all the words of this law."

    (Exodus 34:7; Psalm 5:4–6; Nahum 1:2; Romans 1:18; Ephesians 5:6; Hebrews 9:27; Deuteronomy 27:26; Galatians 3:10)

    Date: _____

11. **But isn't God also merciful?**

God is certainly merciful, but He is also just. His justice demands that sin, committed against His supreme majesty, be punished with the supreme penalty—eternal punishment of body and soul.

(Exodus 34:6, 7; Psalm 103:8, 9; Exodus 34:7; Deuteronomy 7:9–11; Psalm 5:4–6; Hebrews 10:30, 31; Matthew 25:35–46)

Date: _____

12. **According to God's righteous judgment we deserve punishment both in this world and forever after: how can we escape this punishment and return to God's favor?**

God requires that His justice be satisfied. Therefore the claims of His justice must be paid in full, either by ourselves or by another.

(Exodus 23:7; Romans 2:1–11; Isaiah 53:11; Romans 8:3, 4)

Date: _____

13. **Can we pay this debt ourselves?**

Certainly not. Actually, we increase our guilt every day.

(Matthew 6:12; Romans 2:4, 5)

Date: _____

14. **Can another creature–any at all– pay this debt for us?**

No. To begin with, God will not punish another creature for man's guilt. Besides, no mere creature can bear the weight of God's eternal anger against sin and release others from it.

(Ezekiel 18:4, 20; Hebrews 2:14–18; Psalm 49:7–9; 130:3)

Date: _____

Heidelberg Catechism: A Baptist Version

15. **What kind of Mediator and Deliverer should we look for then?**

    He must be truly human and truly righteous, yet more powerful than all creatures, that is, He must also be truly God.

    (Romans 1:3; 2 Corinthians 15:21; Hebrews 2:17; Isaiah 53:9; 2 Corinthians 5:21; Hebrews 7:26; Isaiah 7:14; 9:6; Jeremiah 23:6; John 1:1)

    Date: _____

16. **Why must He be truly human and truly righteous?**

    God's justice demands it: man has sinned, man must pay for his sin, but a sinner cannot pay for others.

    (Romans 5:12, 15; 1 Corinthians 15:21; Hebrews 2:14–16; 7:26, 27; 1 Peter 3:18)

    Date: _____

17. **Why must He also be truly God?**

    So that, by the power of His divinity, He might bear the weight of God's anger in His humanity and earn for us and restore to us righteousness and life.

    (Isaiah 53; John 3:16; 2 Corinthians 5:21)

    Date: _____

18. **And who is this Mediator, who is truly God and at the same time truly human and truly righteous?**

    Our Lord Jesus Christ, who was given us to set us completely free and to make us right with God.

    (Matthew 1:21–23; Luke 2:11; 1 Timothy 2:5; 1 Corinthians 1:30)

    Date: _____

19. **How do you come to know this?**

The holy gospel tells me. God Himself began to reveal the gospel already in Paradise; later, He proclaimed it by the holy patriarchs and prophets, and portrayed it by the sacrifices and other ceremonies of the law; finally, He fulfilled it through His own dear Son.

(Genesis 3:15; 22:18; 49:10; Isaiah 53; Jeremiah 23:5, 6; Micah 7:18–20; Acts 10:43; Hebrews 1:1, 2; Leviticus 1–7; John 5:46; Hebrews 10:1–10; Romans 10:4 Galatians 4:4, 5; Colossians 2:17)

Date: _____

20. **Are all men saved through Christ just as all were lost through Adam?**

No. Only those are saved who by true faith are grafted into Christ and by grace receive all His blessings.

(Matthew 7:14; John 3:16, 18, 36: Romans 11:16–21)

Date: _____

21. **What is true faith?**

True faith is not only a knowledge and conviction that everything God reveals in His Word is true; it is also a deep-rooted assurance, created in me by the Holy Spirit through the gospel that, out of sheer grace earned for us by Christ, not only others, but I too, have had my sins forgiven, have been made forever right with God, and have been granted salvation.

(John 17:3, 17; Hebrews 11:1–3; James 2:19; Romans 4:18–21; 5:1; 10:10; Hebrews 4:14–16; Matthew 16:15–17; John 3:5; Acts 16:14; Romans 1:16; 10:17; 1 Corinthians 1:21; Romans 3:21–26; Galatians 2:16; Ephesians 2:8–10; Galatians 2:20; Romans 1:17; Hebrews 10:10)

Date: _____

22. What then must a Christian believe?

Everything God promises us in the gospel. That gospel is summarized for us in the articles of our Christian faith—a creed beyond doubt, and confessed throughout the world.

(Matthew 28:18–20; John 20:30, 31)

Date: _____

23. What are these articles?

I believe in God the Father, almighty, maker of heaven and earth. And in Jesus Christ, His only begotten Son, our Lord; who was conceived by the Holy Spirit, born of the virgin Mary; suffered under Pontius Pilate; was crucified, dead and buried; He descended into hell; the third day He rose again from the dead; He ascended into heaven, and sitteth at the right hand of God the Father almighty; from there He shall come to judge the living and the dead. I believe in the Holy Spirit; I believe a holy universal church, the communion of saints; the forgiveness of sins; the resurrection of the body; and the life everlasting.

Date: _____

24. How are these articles divided?

Into three parts: God the Father and our creation; God the Son and our deliverance; God the Holy Spirit and our sanctification.

Date: _____

25. Since there is but one God, why do you speak of three: Father, Son, and Holy Spirit?

Because that is how God has revealed Himself in His Word: these three distinct persons are one, true, eternal God.

(Deuteronomy 6:4; 1 Corinthians 8:4, 6; Matthew 3:16, 17; 28:18, 19; Luke 4:18 [Isaiah 61:1]; John 14:26; 15:26; 2 Corinthians 13:14; Galatians 4:6; Titus 3:5, 6)

Date: _____

26. **What do you believe when you say: "I believe in God the Father, almighty, maker of heaven and earth?**

That the eternal Father of our Lord Jesus Christ, who out of nothing created heaven and earth and everything in them, who still upholds and rules them by His eternal counsel and providence, is my God and Father because of Christ His Son. I trust Him so much that I do not doubt He will provide whatever I need for body and soul, and He will turn to my good whatever adversity He sends me in this sad world. He is able to do this because He is almighty God; He desires to do this because He is a faithful Father.

(Genesis 1 & 2; Exodus 20:11; Psalm 33:6; Isaiah 44:24; 14:15; Psalm 104; Matthew 6:30; 10:29; Ephesians 1:11; John 1:12, 13; Romans 8:15, 16; Galatians 4:4–7; Ephesians 1:5; Psalm 55:22; Matthew 6:25, 26; Luke 12:22–31; Romans 8:28; Genesis 18:14; Romans 8:31–39; Matthew 7:9–11)

Date: _____

27. **What do you understand by the providence of God?**

Providence is the almighty and ever present power of God by which He upholds, as with His hand, heaven and earth and all creatures, and so rules them that leaf and blade, rain and drought, fruitful and lean years, food and drink, health and sickness, prosperity and poverty—all things, in fact, come to us not by chance but from His fatherly hand.

(Jeremiah 23:23, 24; Acts 17:24–28; Hebrews 1:3; Jeremiah 5:24; Acts 14:15–17; John 9:3; Proverbs 22:2; 16:33; Matthew 10:29)

Date: _____

28. **How does the knowledge of God's creation and providence help us?**

We can be patient when things go against us, thankful when things go well, and for the future we can have good confidence in our faithful God and Father that nothing will separate us from His love. All creatures are so completely in His hand that without His will they can neither move nor be moved.

(Job 1:21, 22; James 1:3; Deuteronomy 8:10; 1 Thessalonians 5:18; Psalm 55:22; Romans 5:3–5; 8:38, 39; Job 1:12; 2:6; Proverbs 21:1; Acts 17:24–28)

Date: _____

29. **Why is the Son of God called "Jesus" meaning "Savior"?**

Because He saves us from our sins. Salvation cannot be found in anyone else; it is futile to look for any salvation elsewhere.

(Matthew 1:21; Hebrews 7:25; Isaiah 43:11; John 15:5; Acts 4:11, 12; 1 Timothy 2:5)

Date: _____

30. **Do those who look for their salvation and security in saints, in themselves, or elsewhere really believe in the only Savior Jesus?**

No. Although they boast of being His, by their deeds they deny the only Savior and Deliverer, Jesus. Either Jesus is not a perfect Savior, or those who in true faith accept this Savior have in Him all they need for their salvation.

(1 Corinthians 1:12, 13; Galatians 5:4; Colossians 1:19, 20; 2:10; 1 John 1:7)

Date: _____

31. **Why is He called "Christ" meaning "Anointed"?**

Because He has been ordained by God the Father and has been anointed with the Holy Spirit to be our chief Prophet and Teacher who perfectly reveals to us the secret counsel and will of God for our deliverance; our only High Priest who has set us free by the one sacrifice of His body, and who continually pleads our cause with the Father; and our eternal King who governs us by His Word and Spirit, and who guards us and keeps us in the freedom He has won for us.

(Luke 3:21, 22; 4:14–19 [Isaiah 61:1]; Hebrews 1:9 [Psalm 45:7]; Acts 3:22 [Deuteronomy 18:15]; John 1:18; 15:15; Hebrews 7:17 [Psalm 110:4]; Hebrews 9:12; 10:11–14; Romans 8:34; Hebrews 9:24; Matthew 21:5 [Zechariah 9:9]; Matthew 28:18–20; John 10:28; Revelation 12:10, 11)

Date: _____

32. But why are you called a Christian?

Because by faith I am a member of Christ and so I share in His anointing. I am anointed to confess His name, to present myself to Him as a living sacrifice of thanks, to strive with a good conscience against sin and the devil in this life, and afterward to reign with Christ over all creation for all eternity.

(1 Corinthians 12:12–29; Acts 2:17 [Joel 2:28]; 1 John 2:27; Matthew 10:32; Romans 10:9, 10; Hebrews 13:15; Romans 12:1; 1 Peter 2:5, 9; Galatians 5:16, 17; Ephesians 6:11; 1 Timothy 1:18, 19; Matthew 25:34; 2 Timothy 2:12)

Date: _____

33. Why is He called God's "only begotten Son" when we also are God's children?

Because Christ alone is the eternal, natural Son of God. We, however, are adopted children of God—adopted by grace through Christ.

(John 1:1–3, 14, 18; Hebrews 1; John 1:12; Romans 8:14–17; Ephesians 1:5, 6)

Date: _____

34. **Why do you call Him Lord?**

Because—not with gold or silver, but with His precious blood—He has set us free from sin and from the tyranny of the devil, and has bought us, body and soul, to be His very own.

(1 Peter 1:18, 19; Colossians 1:13, 14; Hebrews 2:14, 15; 1 Corinthians 6:20; 1 Timothy 2:5, 6)

Date: _____

35. **What does it mean that He "was conceived by the Holy Spirit, born of the virgin Mary"?**

That the eternal Son of God, who is and remains true and eternal God, took to Himself, through the working of the Holy Spirit, from the flesh and blood of the virgin Mary, a truly human nature so that He might become David's true descendant, in all things like us except for sin.

(John 1:1; 10:30–36; Acts 13:33 [Psalm 2:7]; Colossians 1:15–17; 1 John 5:20; Luke 1:35; Matthew 1:18–23; John 1:14; Galatians 4:4; Hebrews 2:14; 2 Samuel 7:12–16; Psalm 132:11; Matthew 1:1; Romans 1:3; Philippians 2:7; Hebrews 2:17; Hebrews 4:15; 7:26,27)

Date: _____

36. **How does the holy conception and birth of Christ benefit you?**

He is our Mediator, and with His innocence and perfect holiness He removes from God's sight my sin—mine since I was conceived.

(1 Timothy 2:5, 6; Hebrews 9:13–15; Romans 8:3, 4; 2 Corinthians 5:21; Galatians 4:4, 5; 1 Peter 1:18, 19)

Date: _____

37. **What do you understand by the word "suffered"?**
That during His whole life on earth, but especially at the end, Christ sustained in body and soul the anger of God against the sin of the whole human race. This He did in order that, by His suffering as the only atoning sacrifice, He might set us free, body and soul, from eternal condemnation, and gain for us God's grace, righteousness, and eternal life.

(Isaiah 53; 1 Peter 2:24; 3:18; Romans 3:25; Hebrews 10:14; 1 John 2:2; 4:10; Romans 8:1–4; Galatians 3:13; John 3:16; Romans 3:24–26)

Date: _____

38. **Why did He suffer "under Pontius Pilate" as judge?**
So that He, though innocent, might be condemned by a civil judge, and so free us from the severe judgment of God that was to fall on us.

(Luke 23:13–24; John 19:4, 12–16; Isaiah 53:4, 5; 2 Corinthians 5:21; Galatians 3:13)

Date: _____

39. **Is it significant that He was "crucified" instead of dying some other way?**
Yes. This death convinces me that He shouldered the curse which lay on me, since death by crucifixion was accursed by God.

(Galatians 3:10–13 [Deuteronomy 21:23])

Date: _____

40. **Why did Christ have to go all the way to death?**
Because God's justice and truth demand it: only the death of God's Son could pay for our sins.

(Genesis 2:17; Romans 8:3, 4; Philippians 2:8; Hebrews 2:9)

Date: _____

41. **Why was He "buried"?**
His burial testifies that He really died.

(Isaiah 53:9; John 19:38–42; Acts 13:29; 1 Corinthians 15:3, 4)

Date: _____

42. **Since Christ has died for us, why do we still have to die?**
Our death does not pay the debt of our sins. Rather, it puts an end to our sinning and is our entrance into eternal life.

(Psalm 49:7; John 5:24; Philippians 1:21–23; 1 Thessalonians 5:9, 10)

Date: _____

43. **What further advantage do we receive from Christ's sacrifice and death on the cross?**
Through Christ's death our old selves are crucified, put to death, and buried with Him, so that the evil desires of the flesh may no longer rule us, but that instead we may dedicate ourselves as an offering of gratitude to Him.

(Romans 6:5–11; Colossians 2:11, 12; Romans 6:12–14; Romans 12:1; Ephesians 5:1, 2)

Date: _____

44. **How does Christ's resurrection benefit us?**
First, by His resurrection He has overcome death, so that He might make us share in the righteousness He won for us by His death; second, by His power we too are already now resurrected to a new life; third, Christ's resurrection is a guarantee of our glorious resurrection.

(Romans 4:25; 1 Corinthians 15:16–20; 1 Peter 1:3–5; Romans 6:5–11; Ephesians 2:4–6; Colossians 3:1–4; Romans 8:11; 1 Corinthians 15:12–23; Phil. 3:20, 21)

Date: _____

45.   What do you mean by saying: "He ascended into heaven"?

That Christ, while His disciples watched, was lifted up from the earth into heaven and will be there for our good until He comes again to judge the living and the dead.

(Luke 24:50, 51; Acts 1:9–11; Romans 8:34; Ephesians 4:8–18; Hebrews 7:23–25; 9:24; Acts 1:11)

Date: _____

46.   But isn't Christ with us until the end of the world as He promised us?

Christ is true man and true God. In His human nature Christ is not now on earth; but in His divinity, majesty, grace, and Spirit He is not absent from us for a moment.

(Matthew 28:20; Acts 1:9–11; 3:19–21; Matthew 28:18–20; John 14:16–19)

Date: _____

47.   If His humanity is not present wherever His divinity is, then aren't the two natures of Christ separated from each other?

Certainly not. Since divinity is not limited and is present everywhere, it is evident that Christ's divinity is surely beyond the bounds of the humanity He has taken on, but at the same time His divinity is in and remains personally united to His humanity.

(Jeremiah 23:23, 24; Acts 7:48, 49 [Isaiah 66:1]; John 1:14; 3:13; Colossians 2:9)

Date: _____

48.   How does Christ's ascension into heaven benefit us?

First, He pleads our cause in heaven in the presence of His Father; second, we have our own flesh in heaven—a guarantee that Christ our head will take us, His members, to Himself in heaven; third, He sends His Spirit to us on earth as further guarantee. By the Spirit's power we make the goal of our lives, not earthly things, but the things above where Christ is, sitting at God's right hand.

(Romans 8:34; 1 John 2:1; John 14:2; 17:24; Ephesians 2:4–6; John 14:16; 2 Corinthians 1:21, 22; 5:5; Colossians 3:1–4)

Date: _____

49. **Why the next words: "and sits at the right hand of God"?**
Christ ascended to heaven, there to show that He is head of His church, and that the Father rules all things through Him.

(Ephesians 1:20–23; Colossians 1:18; Matthew 28:18; John 5:22, 23)

Date: _____

50. **How does this glory of Christ our head benefit us?**
First, through His Holy Spirit He pours out His gifts from heaven upon us His members; second, by His power He defends us and keeps us safe from all enemies.

(Acts 2:33; Ephesians 4:7–12; Psalm 110:1, 2; John 10:27–30; Revelation 19:11–16)

Date: _____

51. **How does Christ's return "to judge the living and the dead" comfort you?**
In all my distress and persecution I turn my eyes to the heavens and confidently await as judge the very One who has already stood trial in my place before God and so removed the whole curse from me. All His enemies and mine He will condemn to everlasting punishment: but me and all His chosen ones He will take along with Him into the joy and the glory of heaven.

(Luke 21:28; Romans 8:22–25; Philippians 3:20, 21; Titus 2:13, 14; Matthew 25:31–46; 2 Thessalonians 1:6–10)

Date: _____

52. **What do you believe concerning "the Holy Spirit"?**

First, He, as well as the Father and the Son, is eternal God; second, He has been given to me personally, so that, by true faith, He makes me share in Christ and all His blessings, comforts me, and remains with me forever.

(Genesis 1:1, 2; Matthew 28:19; Acts 5:3, 4; 1 Corinthians 6:19; 2 Corinthians 1:21, 22; Galatians 4:6; 3:14; John 15:26; Acts 9:31; John 14:16, 17; 1 Peter 4:14)

Date: _____

53. **What do you believe concerning the "Holy Catholic Church"?**

I believe that the Son of God through His Spirit and Word, out of the entire human race, from the beginning of the world to its end, gathers, protects, and preserves for Himself a community chosen for eternal life and united in true faith. And of this community I am and always will be a living member.

(John 10:14–16; Acts 20:28; Romans 10:14–17; Colossians 1:18; Genesis 26:3b, 4; Revelation 5:9; Isaiah 59:21; 1 Corinthians 11:26; Matthew 16:18; John 10:28–30; Romans 8:28–30; Ephesians 1:3–14; Acts 2:42–47; Ephesians 4:1–6; 1 John 3:14, 19–21; John 10:27, 28; 1 Corinthians 1:4–9; 1 Peter 1:3–5)

Date: _____

54. **What do you understand by "the communion of saints"?**

First, that believers one and all, as members of this community, share in Christ and in all His treasures and gifts; second, that each member should consider it his duty to use his gifts readily and cheerfully for the service and enrichment of the other members.

(Romans 8:32; 1 Corinthians 6:17; 12:4–7, 12, 13; 1 John 1:3; Romans 12:4–8; 1 Corinthians 12:20–27; 13:1–7; Philippians 2:4–8)

Date: _____

55. What do you believe concerning "the forgiveness of sins"?

I believe that God because of Christ's atonement, will never hold against me any of my sins nor my sinful nature which I need to struggle against all my life. Rather, in His grace God grants me the righteousness of Christ to free me forever from judgment.

(Psalm 103:3, 4, 10, 12; Micah 7:18, 19; 2 Corinthians 5:18–21; 1 John 1:7; 2:2; Romans 7:21–25; John 3:17, 18; Romans 8:1, 2)

Date: _____

56. How does "the resurrection of the body" comfort you?

Not only my soul will be taken immediately after this life to Christ its head, but even my very flesh, raised by the power of Christ, will be reunited with my soul and made like Christ's glorious body.

(Luke 23:43; Philippians 1:21–23; 1 Corinthians 15:20, 42–46, 54; Philippians 3:21; 1 John 3:2)

Date: _____

57. How does the article concerning "life everlasting" comfort you?

Even as I already now experience in my heart the beginning of eternal joy, so after this life I will have perfect blessedness such as no eye has seen, no ear heard, no man has ever imagined: a blessedness in which to praise God eternally.

(Romans 14:17; John 17:3; 1 Corinthians 2:9)

Date: _____

58. What good does it do you, however, to believe all this?

In Christ I am right with God and heir to life everlasting.

(John 3:36; Romans 1:17 [Habakkuk 2:4]; Romans 5:1, 2)

Date: _____

59. How are you right with God?

Only by true faith in Jesus Christ. Even though my conscience accuses me of having grievously sinned against all God's commandments and of never having kept any of them, and even though I am still inclined toward all evil, nevertheless, without my deserving it at all, out of sheer grace, God grants and credits to me the perfect satisfaction, righteousness, and holiness of Christ, as if I had never sinned nor been a sinner, as if I had been as perfectly obedient as Christ was obedient for me. All I need to do is to receive this gift of God with a repentant and believing heart.

(Romans 3:21–28; Galatians 2:16; Ephesians 2:8, 9; Philippians 3:8–11; Romans 3:9, 10; 7:23; Titus 3:4, 5; Romans 3:24; Ephesians 2:8; Romans 4:3–5 [Genesis 15:6]; 2 Corinthians 5:17–19; 1 John 2:1, 2; Romans 4:24, 25; 2 Corinthians 5:21; John 3:18; Acts 16:30, 31)

Date: _____

60. Why do you say that by faith alone you are right with God?

It is not because of any value my faith has that God is pleased with me. Only Christ's satisfaction, righteousness, and holiness make me right with God. And I can receive this righteousness and make it mine in no other way than by faith alone.

(1 Corinthians 1:30, 31; Romans 10:10; 1 John 5:10–12)

Date: _____

61. Why can't the good we do make us right with God, or at least help make us right with Him?

Because the righteousness which can pass God's scrutiny must be entirely perfect and must in every way measure up to the divine law. Even the very best we do in this life is imperfect and stained with sin.

(Romans 3:20; Galatians 3:10 [Deuteronomy 27:26]; Isaiah 64:6)

Date: _____

62. **How can you say that the good we do doesn't earn anything when God promises to reward it in this life and the next?**
This reward is not earned; it is a gift of grace.

(Matthew 5:12; Hebrews 11:6; Luke 17:10; 2 Timothy 4:7, 8)

Date: _____

63. **But doesn't this teaching make people indifferent and wicked?**
No. It is impossible for those grafted into Christ by true faith not to produce fruits of gratitude.

(Luke 6:43–45; John 15:5)

Date: _____

64. **You confess that by faith alone you share in Christ and all His blessings: where does faith come from?**
The Holy Spirit produces it in our hearts by the preaching of the holy gospel, confirms it through our use of the holy sacraments, and strengthens it through prayer and Scripture reading.

(John 3:5; 1 Corinthians 2:10–14; Ephesians 2:8; Romans 10:17; 1 Peter 1:23–25; Matthew 28:19, 20; 1 Corinthians 10:16; Ephesians 3:14–21; 1 Peter 2:1–2)

Date: _____

65. **What are sacraments (or ordinances)?**
Sacraments (or ordinances) are holy signs for believers. They were instituted by God so that by our use of them He might make us understand more clearly the promise of the gospel. And this is God's gospel promise: to forgive our sins and give us eternal life by grace alone because of Christ's one sacrifice finished on the cross.

(Genesis 17:11; Deuteronomy 30:6; Romans 4:11; Matthew 26:27, 28; Hebrews 10:10; Acts 2:38)

Date: _____

66. **Are both the Word and the sacraments then intended to focus our faith on the sacrifice of Jesus Christ on the cross as the only ground of our salvation?**
Right! In the gospel the Holy Spirit teaches us and through the holy sacraments He assures us that our entire salvation rests on Christ's one sacrifice for us on the cross.
(Romans 6:3; 1 Corinthians 11:26; Galatians 3:27)

Date: _____

67. **How many sacraments did Christ institute in the New Testament?**
Two: baptism and the Lord's supper.
(Matthew 28:19, 20; 1 Corinthians 23:26)

Date: _____

68. **What is Baptism?**
Baptism is the immersion of a believer into water as a sign of his union with Jesus Christ and salvation by God's grace.
(Matthew 28:19; Acts 8:36–39)

Date: _____

69. **What does baptism symbolize?**
My death, burial and resurrection with the Lord Jesus Christ.
(Romans 6:1–4)

Date: _____

70. **Who should be baptized?**
Those who, having been born of God's Spirit, repent of their sins and believe in Jesus Christ for salvation. In other words, only believers should be baptized.
(Acts 2:41–42; Matthew 28:19)

Date: _____

71. What is the Lord's Supper?

The Lord's Supper is the declaration of Christ's death by believers through the giving and receiving of bread and the fruit of the vine.

(1 Corinthians 11:23–26; Luke 22)

Date: _____

72. How does the Lord's supper remind you and assure you that you share in Christ's one sacrifice on the cross and in all His gifts?

In this way: Christ has commanded me and all believers to eat this broken bread and to drink this cup. With this command He gave this promise: First, as surely as I see with my eyes the bread of the Lord broken for me and the cup given to me, so surely His body was offered and broken for me on the cross. Second, as surely as I receive from the hand of him who serves, and taste with my mouth the bread and cup of the Lord, given me as sure signs of Christ's body and blood, so surely He nourishes and refreshes my soul for eternal life with His crucified body and poured-out blood.

(Matthew 26:26–28; Mark 14:22–24; Luke 22:19, 20; 1 Corinthians 11:23–25)

Date: _____

73. Are the bread and fruit of the vine changed into the real body and blood of Christ?

No. Just as the water of baptism is not changed into Christ's blood and does not itself wash away sins but is a sign of our union with Christ, so too the bread and fruit of the vine of the Lord's supper are not changed into the actual body and blood of Christ in keeping with the nature and language of sacraments.

(Ephesians 5:26; Titus 3:5; Matthew 26:26–29; 1 Corinthians 10:16, 17; 11:26–28; Genesis 17:10, 11; Exodus 12:11; 1 Corinthians 10:1–4)

Date: _____

74. Why then does Christ call the bread His body and the cup His blood, or the new covenant in His blood?

Christ has good reason for these words. He wants to teach us that He established the new covenant by His death and that as bread and drink nourish our temporal life, so too His crucified body and poured-out blood truly nourish our souls for eternal life. But more important, He wants to assure us, by this visible sign and pledge, that we, through the Holy Spirit's work, share in His true body and blood as surely as our mouths receive these holy signs in His remembrance, and that all of His suffering and obedience are as definitely ours as if we personally had suffered and paid for our sins.

(John 6:51, 55; 1 Corinthians 10:16,17; 11:26; Romans 6:5–11)

Date: _____

75. Who are to come to the Lord's table?

Those baptized believers who are displeased with themselves because of their sins, but who nevertheless trust that their sins are pardoned and that their continuing weakness is covered by the suffering and death of Christ, and who also desire more and more to strengthen their faith and to lead a better life. Hypocrites and those who are unrepentant, however, eat and drink judgment on themselves.

(1 Corinthians 10:19–22; 11:26–32)

Date: _____

76. Are those who show by what they say and do that they are unbelieving and ungodly to be admitted to the Lord's supper?

No, that would dishonor God's covenant and bring down God's anger upon the entire congregation. Therefore, according to the instruction of Christ and His apostles, the Christian church is duty-bound to exclude such people, by the official use of the keys of the kingdom, until they repent of their sins.

(1 Corinthians 11:17–32; Psalm 50:14–16; Isaiah 1:11–17)

Date: _____

77. What are the keys of the kingdom?

The preaching of the holy gospel and Christian discipline toward repentance. Both preaching and discipline open the kingdom of heaven to believers and close it to unbelievers.

(Matthew 16:19; John 20:22, 23)

Date: _____

78. How does preaching the gospel open and close the kingdom of heaven?

According to the command of Christ: The kingdom of heaven is opened by proclaiming and publicly declaring to each and every believer that, as often as he accepts the gospel promise in true faith, God, because of what Christ has done, truly forgives all his sins. The kingdom of heaven is closed, however, by proclaiming and publicly declaring to unbelievers and hypocrites that, as long as they do not repent, the anger of God and eternal condemnation rest on them. God's judgment, both in this life and in the life to come, is based on this gospel testimony.

(Matthew 16:19; John 3:31–36; 20:21–23)

Date: _____

79. How is the kingdom of heaven closed and opened by Christian discipline?

According to the command of Christ: If anyone, though called a Christian, professes unchristian teachings or lives an unchristian life, if after repeated brotherly counsel, he refuses to abandon his errors and wickedness, and, if after being reported to the church he fails to respond also to their admonition—such a one the church must exclude from the Christian fellowship and God Himself excludes him from the kingdom of Christ. Such a person, when he promises and demonstrates genuine repentance, is received again as a member of Christ and of His church.

(Matthew 18:15–20; 1 Corinthians 5:3–5, 11–13; 2 Thessalonians 3:14, 15; Luke 15:20–24; 2 Corinthians 2:6–11)

Date: _____

80. **We have been delivered from our misery by God's grace alone through Christ and not because we have earned it: Why then must we still do good?**
To be sure, Christ has redeemed us by His blood. But we do good because Christ by His Spirit is also renewing us to be like Himself, so that in all our living we may show that we are thankful to God for all He has done for us, and so that He may be praised through us. And we do good so that we may be assured of our faith by its fruits, and so that by our godly living our neighbors may be won over to Christ.

(Romans 6:13; 12:1, 2; 1 Peter 2:5–10; Matthew 5:16; 1 Corinthians 6:19, 20; Matthew 7:17, 18; Galatians 5:22–24; 2 Peter 1:10, 11; Matthew 5:14–16; Romans 14:17–19; 1 Peter 2:12; 3:1, 2)

Date: _____

81. **Can those be saved who do not turn to God from their ungrateful and impenitent ways?**
By no means. Scripture tells us that no unchaste person, no idolater, adulterer, thief, no covetous person, no drunkard, slanderer, robber, or the like is going to inherit the kingdom of God.

(1 Corinthians 6:9, 10; Galatians 5:19–21; Ephesians 5:1–20; 1 John 3:14)

Date: _____

82. **What is involved in genuine repentance or conversion?**
Two things: the dying-away of the old self, and the coming-to-life of the new.

(Romans 6:1–11; 2 Corinthians 5:17; Ephesians 4:22–24; Colossians 3:5–10)

Date: _____

83. **What is the dying-away of the old self?**
It is to be genuinely sorry for sin, to hate it more and more, and to run away from it.

(Psalm 51:3, 4, 17; Joel 2:12, 13; Romans 8:12, 13; 2 Corinthians 7:10)

Date: _____

84. **What is the coming-to-life of the new self?**
It is a wholehearted joy in God through Christ and a delight to do every kind of good as God wants us to.

(Psalm 51:8, 12; Isaiah 57:15; Romans 5:1; 14:17; 6:10, 11; Galatians 2:20)

Date: _____

85. **What do we do that is good?**
Only that which arises out of true faith, conforms to God's law, and is done for His glory; and not that which is based on what we think is right or on established human tradition.

(John 15:5; Hebrews 11:6; Leviticus 18:4 1 Samuel 15:22; Ephesians 2:10; 1 Corinthians 10:31; Deuteronomy 12:32; Isaiah 29:13; Ezekiel 20:18, 19; Matthew 15:7–9)

Date: _____

86. What does the Lord say in His law?

God spoke all these words:

I am the Lord your God, who brought you out of the land of Egypt, out of the house of bondage. You shall have no other gods before Me.

You shall not make for yourself a graven image, or any likeness of anything that is in heaven above, or that is in the earth beneath, or that is in the water under the earth; you shall not bow down to them or serve them; for I the Lord your God am a jealous God, visiting the iniquity of the fathers upon the children to the third and the fourth generation of those who hate Me, but showing steadfast love to thousands of those who love Me and keep My commandments.

You shall not take the name of the Lord your God in vain; for the Lord will not hold him guiltless who takes His name in vain.

Remember the Sabbath day, to keep it holy. Six days you shall labor, and do all your work; but the seventh day is a Sabbath to the Lord your God; in it you shall not do any work, you, or your son, or your daughter, your manservant, or your maidservant, or your cattle, or the sojourner who is within your gates; for in six days the Lord made heaven and earth, the sea, and all that is in them, and rested the seventh day; therefore the Lord blessed the Sabbath day and hallowed it.

Honor your father and your mother, that your days may be long in the land which the Lord your God gives you.

You shall not kill.

You shall not commit adultery.

You shall not steal.

You shall not bear false witness against your neighbor.

You shall not covet your neighbor's house; you shall not covet your neighbor's wife, or his manservant, or his maidservant, or his ox, or his ass, or anything that is your neighbor's.

(Exodus 20:1–17; Deuteronomy 5:6–21)

Date: _____

87. How are these commandments divided?

Into two tables. The first has four commandments, teaching us what our relation to God should be. The second has six commandments, teaching us what we owe our neighbor.

(Matthew 22:37–39)

Date: _____

88. What does the Lord require in the first commandment?

That I, not wanting to endanger my very salvation, avoid and shun all idolatry, magic, superstitious rites, and prayer to saints or the other creatures. That I sincerely acknowledge the only true God, trust Him alone, look to Him for every good thing humbly and patiently, love Him, fear Him, and honor Him with all my heart. In short, that I give up anything rather than go against His will in any way.

(1 Corinthians 6:9,10; 10:5–14; 1 John 5:21; Leviticus 19:31; Deuteronomy 18:9–12; Matthew 4:10; Revelation 19:10; 22:8, 9; John 17:3; Jeremiah 17: 5, 7; Psalm 104:27, 28; James 1:17; 1 Peter 5:5, 6; Colossians 1:11; Hebrews 10:36; Matthew 2:37 [Deuteronomy 6:50]; Proverbs 9:10; 1 Peter 1:17; Matthew 4:10 [Deuteronomy 6:13]; Matthew 5:29, 30; 10:37–39)

Date: _____

89. What is idolatry?

Idolatry is having or inventing something in which one trusts in place of or alongside of the only true God, who has revealed Himself in His Word.

(1 Chronicles 16:26; Galatians 4:8, 9; Ephesians 5:5; Phil. 3:19)

Date: _____

90. What is God's will for us in the second commandment?

That we in no way make any image of God nor worship Him in any other way than He has commanded in His Word.

(Deuteronomy 4:15–19; Isaiah 40:18–25; Acts 17:29; Romans 1:23; Leviticus 10:1–7; 1 Samuel 15:22, 23; John 4:23, 24)

Date: _____

91. May we then not make any image at all?

God can not and may not be visibly portrayed in any way. Although creatures may be portrayed, yet God forbids making or having such images if one's intention is to worship them or to serve God through them.

(Exodus 34:13, 14, 17; 2 Kings 18:4, 5)

Date: _____

92. But may not images be permitted in the churches as teaching aids for the unlearned?

No, we shouldn't try to be wiser than God. He wants His people instructed by the living preaching of His Word—not by idols that cannot even talk.

(Romans 10:14, 15, 17; 2 Timothy 3:16, 17; 2 Peter 1:19; Jeremiah 10:8; Habakkuk 2:18–20)

Date: _____

93. What is God's will for us in the third commandment?

That we neither blaspheme nor misuse the name of God by cursing, perjury, or unnecessary oaths, nor share in such horrible sins by being silent bystanders. In a word, it requires that we use the holy name of God only with reverence and awe, so that we may properly confess Him, pray to Him, and praise Him in everything we do and say.

(Leviticus 24:10–17; Leviticus 19:12; Matthew 5:37; James 5:12; Leviticus 5:1; Proverbs 29:24; Psalm 99:1–5; Jeremiah 4:2; Matthew 10:32, 33: Romans 10:9, 10; Psalm 50:14, 15; 1 Timothy 2:8; Colossians 3:17)

Date: _____

94. Is blasphemy of God's name by swearing and cursing really such serious sin that God is angry also with those who do not do all they can to help prevent it and to forbid it?

Yes, indeed. No sin is greater, no sin makes God more angry than blaspheming His name. That is why He commanded the death penalty for it.

(Leviticus 5:1; 24:10–17)

Date: _____

95. But may we swear an oath in God's name if we do it reverently?

Yes, when the government demands it, or when necessity requires it, in order to maintain and promote truth and trustworthiness for God's glory and our neighbor's good. Such oaths are approved in God's Word and were rightly used by Old and New Testament believers.

(Deuteronomy 6:13; 10:20; Jeremiah 4:1, 2; Hebrews 6:16; Genesis 21:24; Joshua 9:15; 1 Kings 1:29, 30; Romans 1:9; 2 Corinthians 1:23)

Date: _____

96. May we swear by saints or other creatures?

No. A legitimate oath means calling upon God as the One who knows my heart to witness to my truthfulness and to punish me if I swear falsely. No creature is worthy of such honor.

(Romans 9:1; 2 Corinthians 1:23; Matthew 5:34–37; 23:16–22; James 5:12)

Date: _____

97. What is God's will for us in the fourth commandment?

First, that the gospel ministry and education for it be maintained, and that, especially on the festive day of rest, I regularly attend the assembly of God's people to learn what God's Word teaches, to participate in the sacraments, to pray to God publicly, and to bring Christian offerings for the poor. Second, that every day of my life I rest from my evil ways, let the Lord work in me through His Spirit, and so begin already in this life the eternal Sabbath.

(Deuteronomy 6:4–9, 20–25; 1 Corinthians 9:13, 14; 2 Timothy 2:2; 3:13–17; Titus 1:5; Deuteronomy 12:5–12; Psalm 40:9, 10; 68:26; Acts 2:42–47; Hebrews 10:23–25; Romans 10:14–17; 1 Corinthians 14:31, 32; 1 Timothy 4:13; 1 Corinthians 11:23, 24; Colossians 3:16; 1 Timothy 2:1; Psalm 50:14; 1 Corinthians 16:2; 2 Corinthians 8, 9; Isaiah 66:23; Hebrews 4:9–11)

Date: _____

98. What is God's will for us in the fifth commandment?

That I honor, love, and be loyal to my father and mother and all those in authority over me; that I obey and submit to them, as is proper, when they correct and punish me; and also that I be patient with their failings—for through them God chooses to rule us.

(Exodus 21:17; Proverbs 1:8; 4:1; Romans 13:1, 2; Ephesians 5:21, 22; 6:1–9; Colossians 3:18–4:1; Proverbs 20:20; 23:22; 1 Peter 2:18; Matthew 22:21; Romans 13:1–8; Ephesians 6:1–9; Colossians 3:18–21)

Date: _____

99. What is God's will for us in the sixth commandment?

I am not to belittle, insult, hate, or kill my neighbor—not by my thoughts, my words, my look or gesture, and certainly not by actual deeds—and I am not to be party to this in others; rather, I am to put away all desire for revenge. I am not to harm or recklessly endanger myself either. Prevention of murder is also why government is armed with the sword.

(Genesis 9:6; Leviticus 19:17, 18; Matthew 5:21, 22; 26:52; Proverbs 25:21, 22; Matthew 18:35; Romans 18:35 Ephesians 4:26; Matthew 4:7; 26:52; Romans 13:11–14; Genesis 9:6; Exodus 21:14; Romans 13:4)

Date: _____

100. Does this commandment refer only to killing?

By forbidding murder God teaches us that He hates the root of murder: envy, hatred, anger, vindictiveness. In God's sight all such are murder.

(Proverbs 14:30; Romans 1:29; 12:19; Galatians 5:19–21; 1 John 2:9–11; 3:15)

Date: _____

101. Is it enough then that we do not kill our neighbor in any such way?

No. By condemning envy, hatred, and anger God tells us to love our neighbor as ourselves, to be patient, peace–loving, gentle, merciful, and friendly to him, to protect him from harm as much as we can, and to do good even to our enemies.

(Matthew 7:12; 22:39; Romans 12:10; Matthew 5:3–12; Luke 6:36; Romans 12:10, 18; Galatians 6:1, 2; Ephesians 4:2; Colossians 3:12; 1 Peter 3:8; Exodus 23:4, 5; Matthew 5:44, 45; Romans 12:20, 21 [Proverbs 25:21, 22])

Date: _____

102. What is God's will for us in the seventh commandment?
God condemns all unchastity. We should therefore thoroughly
detest it and, married or single, live decent and chaste lives.

(Leviticus 18:30; Ephesians 5:3–5; Jude 22, 23; 1 Corinthians 7:1–9; 1
Thessalonians 4:3–8; Hebrews 13:4)

Date: _____

**103. Does God, in this commandment, forbid only such
scandalous sins as adultery?**
We are temples of the Holy Spirit, body and soul, and God
wants both to be kept clean and holy. That is why He forbids
everything which incites unchastity, whether it be actions, look,
talk, thoughts, or desires.

(1 Corinthians 15:33; Ephesians 5:18; Matthew 5:27–29; 1 Corinthians
6:18–20; Ephesians 5:3, 4)

Date: _____

104. What does God forbid in the eighth commandment?
He forbids not only outright theft and robbery, punishable
by law. But in God's sight theft also includes cheating and
swindling our neighbor by schemes made to appear legitimate,
such as: inaccurate measurements of weight, size, or volume;
fraudulent merchandising; counterfeit money; excessive
interest; or any other means forbidden by God. In addition He
forbids all greed and pointless squandering of His gifts.

(Exodus 22:1; 1 Corinthians 5:9, 10; 6:9, 10; Micah 6:9–11; Luke 3:14;
James 5:1–6; Deuteronomy 25:13–16; Psalm 15:5; Proverbs 11:1; 12:22;
Ezekiel 45:9–12; Luke 6:35; 12:15; Ephesians 5:5; Proverbs 21:20; 23:20,
21; Luke 16:10–13)

Date: _____

105. What does God require of you in this commandment?

That I do whatever I can for my neighbor's good, that I treat him as I would like others to treat me, and that I work faithfully so that I may share with those in need.

(Isaiah 58:5–10; Matthew 7:12; Galatians 6:9, 10; Ephesians 4:28)

Date: _____

106. What is God's will for us in the ninth commandment?

God's will is that I never give false testimony against anyone, twist no one's words, not gossip or slander, nor join in condemning anyone without a hearing or without a just cause. Rather, in court and everywhere else, I should avoid lying and deceit of every kind; these are devices the devil himself uses, and they would call down on me God's intense anger. I should love the truth, speak it candidly, and openly acknowledge it. And I should do what I can to guard and advance my neighbor's good name.

(Psalm 15; Proverbs 19:5; Matthew 7:1; Luke 6:37; Romans 1:28–32. Leviticus 19:11, 12; Proverbs 12:22; 13:5; John 8:44; Revelation 21:8; 1 Corinthians 13:6; Ephesians 4:25; 1 Peter 3:8, 9; 4:8)

Date: _____

107. What is God's will for us in the tenth commandment?

That not even the slightest thought or desire contrary to any one of God's commandments should ever arise in my heart. Rather, with all my heart I should always hate sin and take pleasure in whatever is right.

(Psalm 19:7–14; 139:23, 24; Romans 7:7, 8)

Date: _____

108. But can those converted to God obey these commandments perfectly?

No. In this life even the holiest have only a small beginning of this obedience. Nevertheless, with all seriousness of purpose, they do begin to live according to all, not only some, of God's commandments.

(Ecclesiastes 7:20; Romans 7:14, 15; 1 Corinthians 13:9; 1 John 1:8–10; Psalm 1:1, 2; Romans 7:22–25; Philippians 3:12–16)

Date: _____

109. No one in this life can obey the ten commandments perfectly: why then does God want them preached so pointedly?

First, so that the longer we live the more we may come to know our sinfulness and the more eagerly look to Christ for forgiveness of sins and righteousness. Second, so that, while praying to God for the grace of the Holy Spirit, we may never stop striving to be renewed more and more after God's image, until after this life we reach our goal: perfection.

(Psalm 32:5; Romans 3:19–26; 7:7, 24, 25; 1 John 1:9; 1 Corinthians 9:24; Philippians 3:12–14; 1 John 3:1–3)

Date: _____

110. Why do Christians need to pray?

Because prayer is the most important part of the thankfulness God requires of us. And also because God gives His grace and Holy Spirit only to those who pray continually and groan inwardly, asking God for these gifts and thanking Him for them.

(Psalm 50:14, 15; 116:12–19; 1 Thessalonians 5:16–18; Matthew 7:7, 8; Luke 11:9–13)

Date: _____

111. How does God want us to pray so that He will listen to us?

First, we must pray from the heart to no other than the one true God, who has revealed Himself in His Word, asking for everything He has commanded us to ask for. Second, we must acknowledge our need and misery, hiding nothing, and humble ourselves in His majestic presence. Third, we must rest on this unshakable foundation: even though we do not deserve it, God will surely listen to our prayer because of Christ our Lord. That is what He promised in His Word.

(Psalm 145:18–20; John 4:22–24; Romans 8:26, 27; James 1:5; 1 John 5:14, 15; 2 Chronicles 7:14; Psalm 2:11; 34:18; 62:8; Isaiah 66:2; Revelation 4; Daniel 9:17–19; Matthew 7:8; John 14:13, 14; 16:23; Romans 10:13; James 1:6)

Date: _____

112. What did God command us to pray for?

Everything we need, spiritually and physically, as embraced in the prayer Christ our Lord Himself taught us.

(James 1:17; Matthew 6:33)

Date: _____

113. What is this prayer?

Our Father in heaven, hallowed be Your name. Your kingdom come, Your will be done on earth as it is in heaven. Give us this day our daily bread. And forgive us our debts as we forgive our debtors. And do not lead us into temptation, but deliver us from the evil one. For Yours is the kingdom and the power and the glory forever. Amen.

(Matthew 6:9–13; Luke 11:2–4)

Date: _____

114. Why did Christ command us to call God, "our Father"?
At the very beginning of our prayer Christ wants to kindle in us what is basic to our prayer—the childlike awe and trust that God through Christ has become our Father. Our fathers do not refuse us the things of this life; God our Father will even less refuse to give us what we ask in faith.

(Matthew 7:9–11; Luke 11:11–13)

Date: _____

115. Why the words, "who art in heaven"?
These word teach us not to think of God's heavenly majesty as something earthly, and to expect everything for body and soul from His almighty power.

(Jeremiah 23:23, 24; Acts 17:24, 25; Matthew 6:25–34; Romans 8:31, 32)

Date: _____

116. What does the first request mean?
Hallowed be Your name means, help us to really know You, to bless, worship, and praise You for all Your works and for all that shines forth from them: Your almighty power, wisdom, kindness, justice, mercy, and truth. And it means, help us to direct all our living—what we think, say, and do—so that Your name will never be blasphemed because of us but always honored and praised.

(Jeremiah 9:23, 24; 31:33, 34; Matthew 16:17; John 17:3; Exodus 34:5–8; Psalm 145; Jeremiah 32:16–20; Luke 1:46–55, 68–75; Romans 11:33–36; Psalm 115:1; Matthew 5:16)

Date: _____

117. What does the second request mean?

Your kingdom come means, rule us by Your Word and Spirit in such a way that more and more we submit to You. Keep Your church strong, and add to it. Destroy the devil's work; destroy every force which revolts against You and every conspiracy against Your Word. Do this until Your kingdom is so complete and perfect that in it You are all in all.

(Matthew 7:21; 16:24–26; Luke 22:42; Romans 12:1, 2; Titus 2:11, 12; 1 Corinthians 7:17–24; Ephesians 6:5–9; Psalm 103:20, 21)

Date: _____

118. What does the fourth request mean?

Give us this day our daily bread means, do take care of all our physical needs so that we come to know that You are the only source of everything good, and that neither our work and worry nor Your gifts can do us any good without Your blessing. And so help us to give up our trust in creatures and to put trust in You alone.

(Psalm 104:27–30; 145:15, 16; Matthew 6:25–34; Acts 14:17; 17:25; James 1:17; Deuteronomy 8:3; Psalm 37:16; 127:1, 2; 1 Corinthians 15:58; Psalm 55:22; 62; 146; Jeremiah 17:5–8; Hebrews 13:5, 6)

Date: _____

119. What does the fifth request mean?

And forgive us our debts, as we also forgive our debtors means, because of Christ's blood, do not hold against us, poor sinners that we are, any of the sins we do or the evil that constantly clings to us. Forgive us just as we are fully determined, as evidence of Your grace in us, to forgive our neighbors.

(Psalm 51:1–7; 143:2; Romans 8:1; 1 John 2:1, 2; Matthew 6:14, 15; 18:21–35)

Date: _____

120. What does the sixth request mean?

And lead us not into temptation, but deliver us from evil means, by ourselves we are too weak to hold our own even for a moment. And our sworn enemies—the devil, the world, and our own flesh—never stop attacking us. And so, Lord, uphold us and make us strong with the strength of Your Holy Spirit, so that we may not go down to defeat in this spiritual struggle, but may firmly resist our enemies until we finally win the complete victory.

(Psalm 103:14–16; John 15:1–5; 2 Corinthians 11:14; Ephesians 6:10–13; 1 Peter 5:8; John 15:18–21; Romans 7:23; Galatians 5:17; Matthew 10:19, 20; 26:41; Mark 13:33; Romans 5:3–5; 1 Corinthians 10:13; 1 Thessalonians 3:13; 5:23)

Date: _____

121. What does your conclusion to this prayer mean?

For Yours is the kingdom, and the power, and the glory, forever means, we have made all these requests of You because, as our all-powerful King, You not only want to, but are able to give us all that is good; and because Your holy name, and not we ourselves, should receive all the praise, forever.

(Romans 10:11–13; 2 Peter 2:9; Psalm 115:1; John 14:13)

Date: _____

122. What does that little word "amen" mean?

Amen means, this is sure to be! It is even more sure that God listens to my prayer, than that I really desire what I pray for.

(Isaiah 65:24; 2 Corinthians 1:20; 2 Timothy 2:13)

Date: _____

CPSIA information can be obtained
at www.ICGtesting.com
Printed in the USA
BVOW08s0252100317
478074BV00001B/28/P